VOLUME 1

¡IMAGINLAB!

IGNITING THE RIGHT-BRAIN

BY A.M. PERKINS

?

HMMM...

AH HA!

A RULE-FREE
COMPLETE-THE-DRAWING WORKBOOK

HOW THIS BOOK WORKS

This is a rule-free, complete-the drawing workbook designed to stimulate and ignite the right-brain and get those creative juices stirred up.

This is not your standard coloring/drawing book. There are no rules. You can turn these sketches into anything your imagination desires from simple drawings to complex illustrations. Transform them into cartoon characters. Doodle on them. Color them. See how many ways you can transform a single doodle. Compare your work with a friend's to see what each of you came up with. The sky is the limit and your imagination is the ride!

Warning: This book can be addicting.

HOW TO USE:

1. Look at the pre-drawn sketch.
2. What do you "see"? (hint: everyone will see something different!)
3. Draw what you see and explore your creativity!

OTHER GREAT USES:

1. Boredom buster for car rides , lengthy office visits or long trips. Don't leave home without it!

2. Use for relaxation as you enjoy tapping into your creative side (eh-hem, I'm speaking to you adults out there!).

3. Use them for family fun nights to see how many variations you can come up with as a family!

ISBN-13: 978-0692765685
ISBN-10: 0692765689

ImaginLab
P.O. Box 63
Yadkinville, NC 27055
www.imagin-lab.com

THESE CREATIONS BELONG TO:

_____

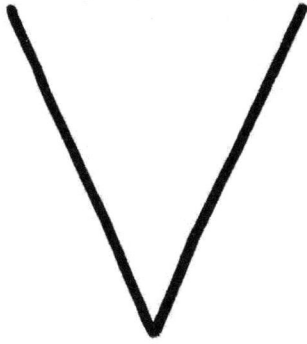

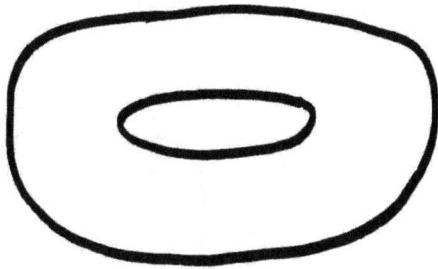

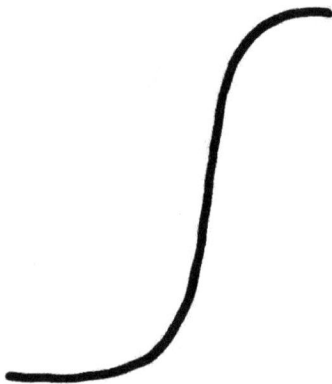

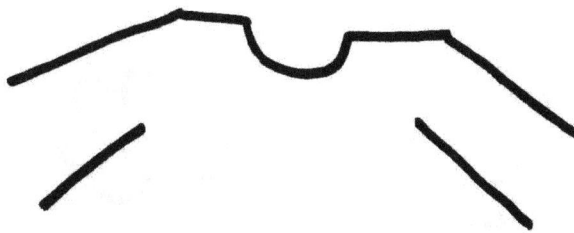

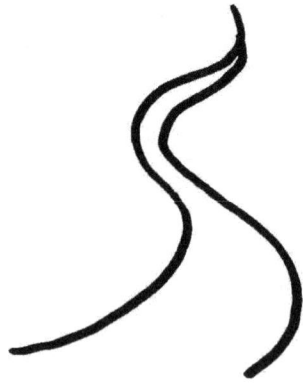

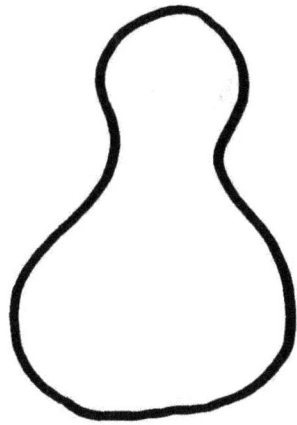

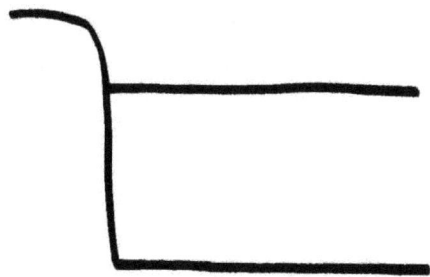

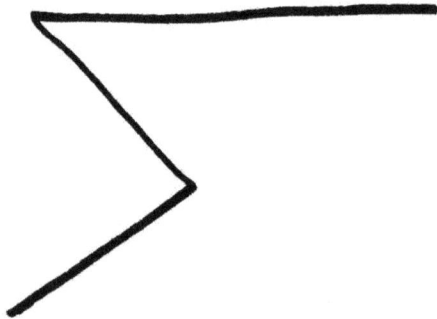

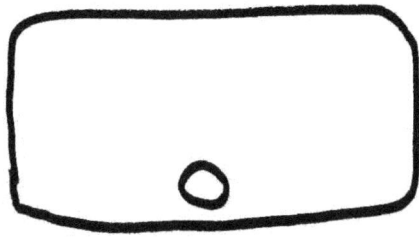

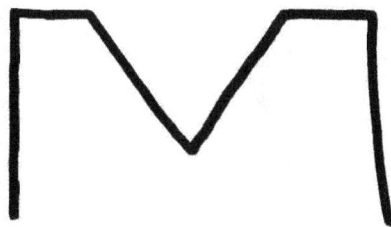

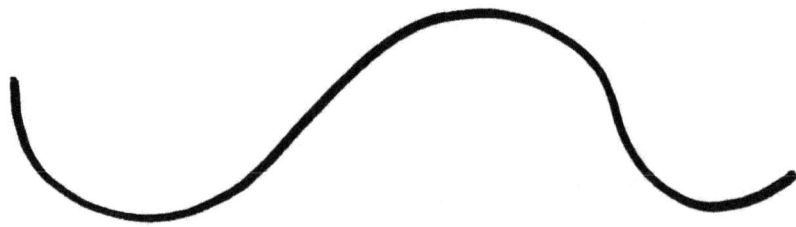

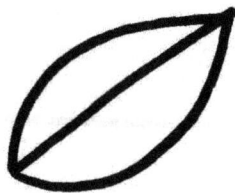

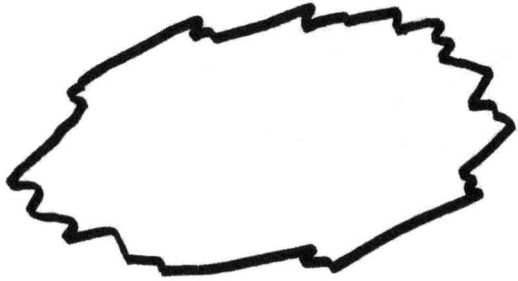

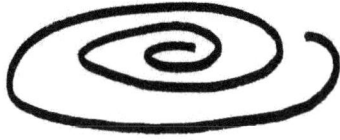

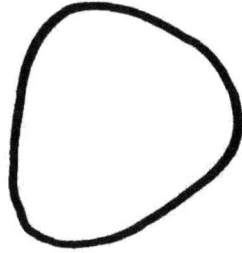

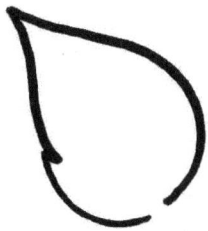

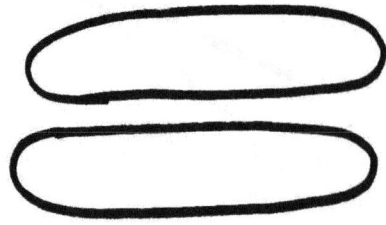

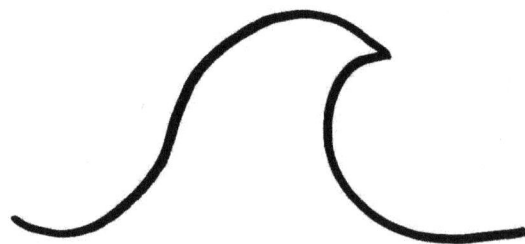

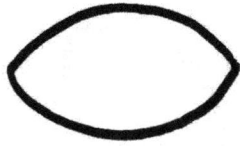

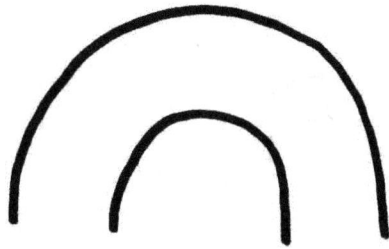

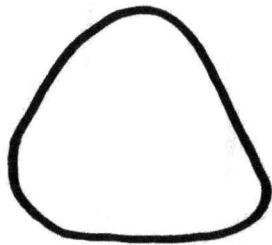

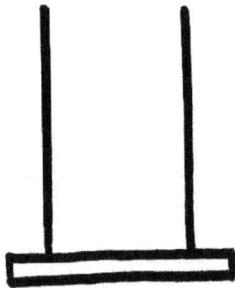

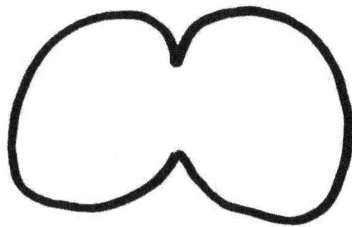

( )

ろ

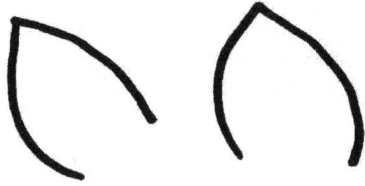

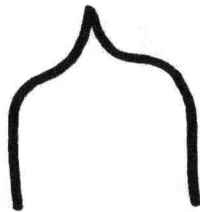

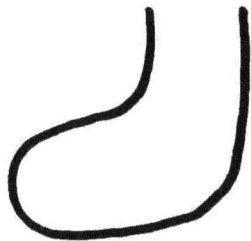

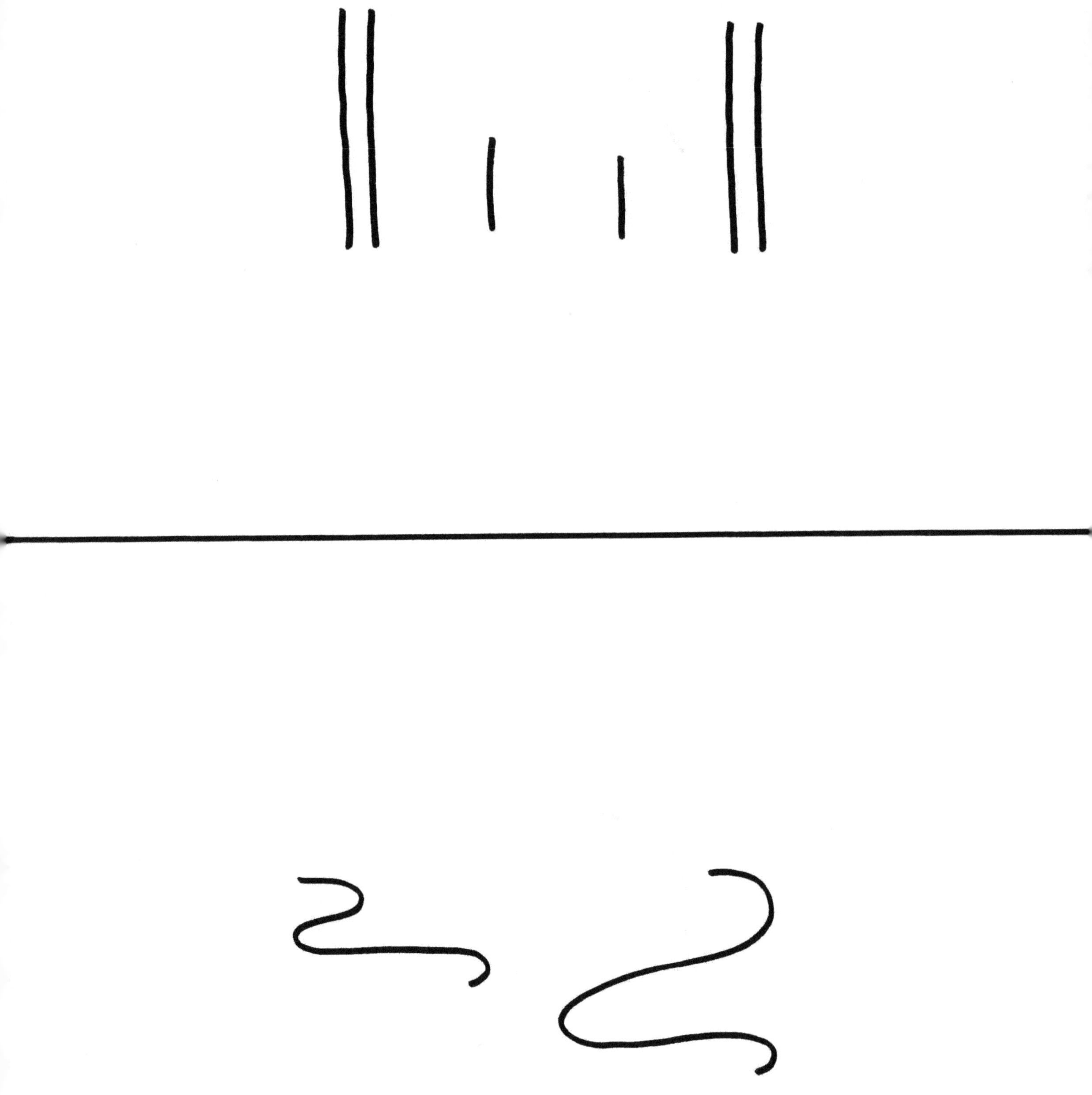

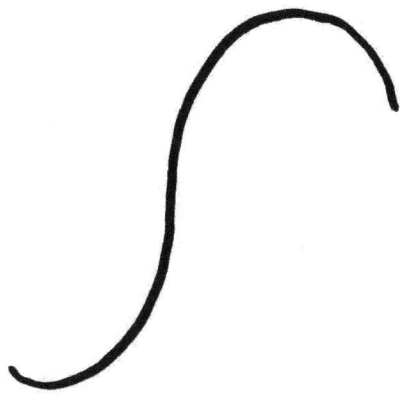

W

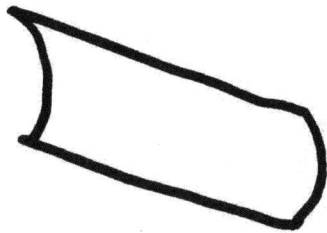

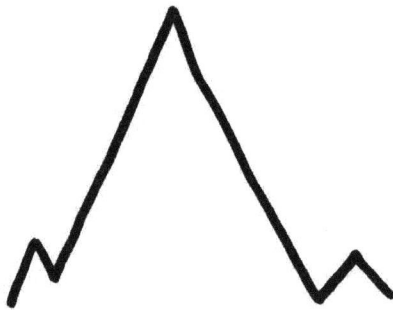

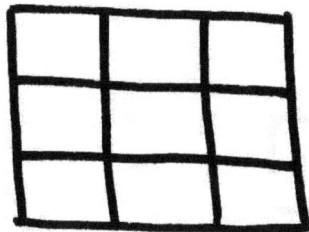

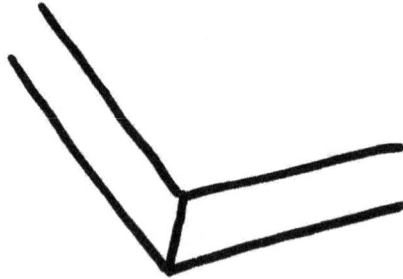

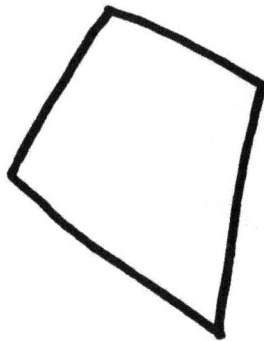

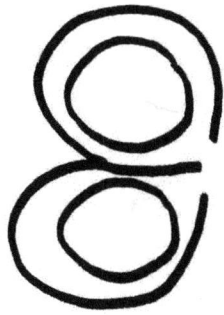

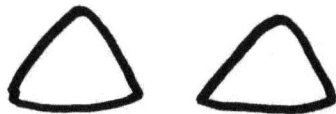

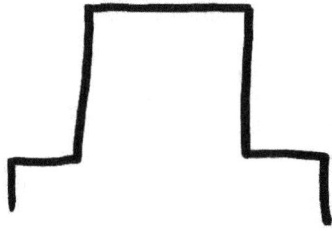

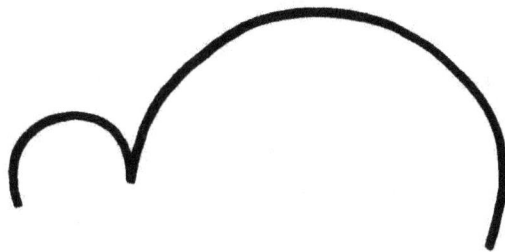

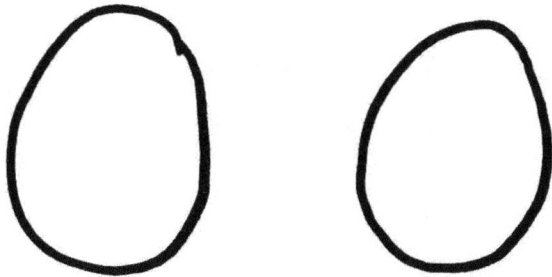

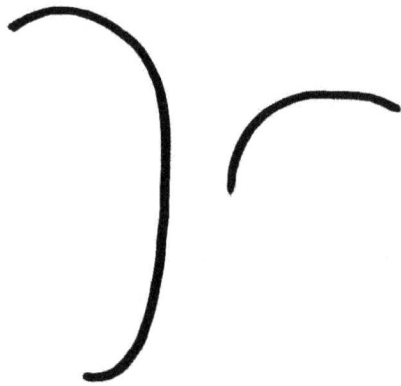

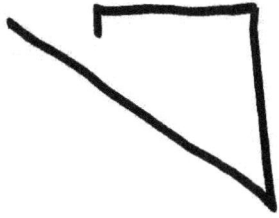

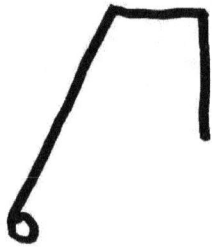

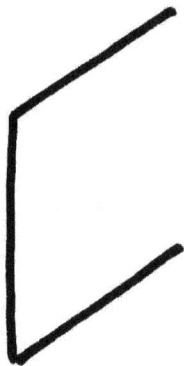

3

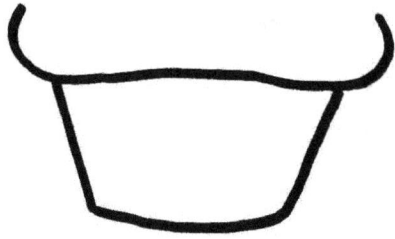

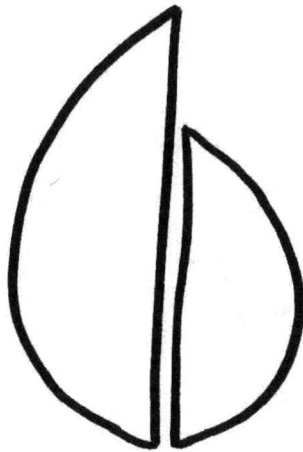

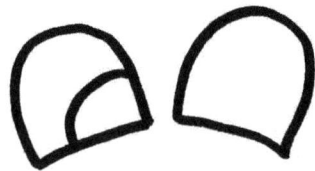

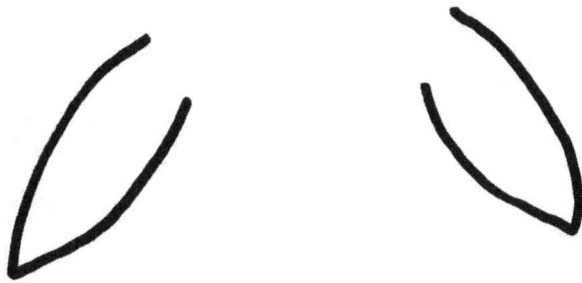

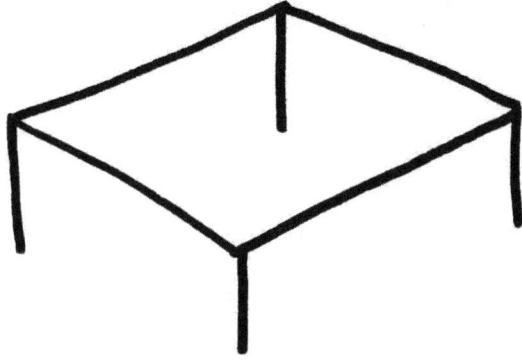

Ooooo

‹⁊ ⁊›

‹⁊

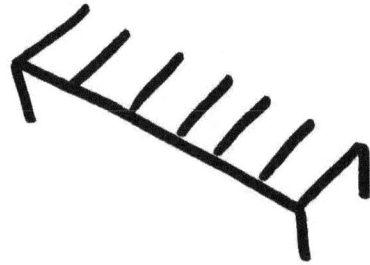

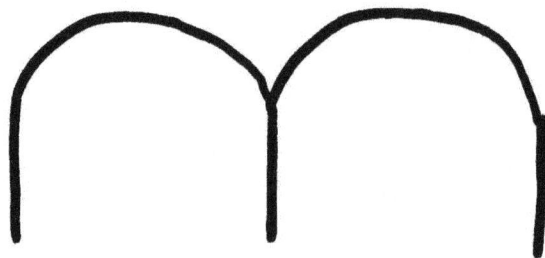

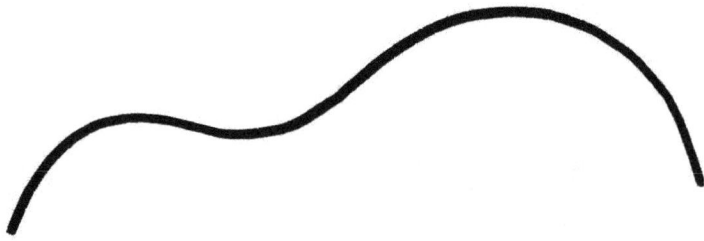

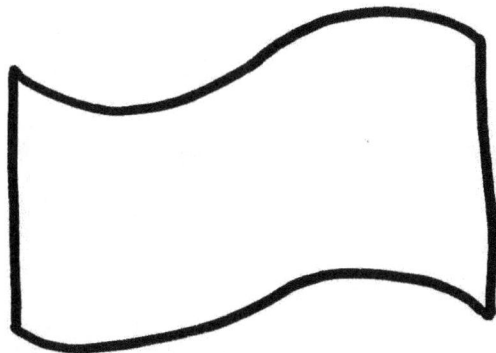

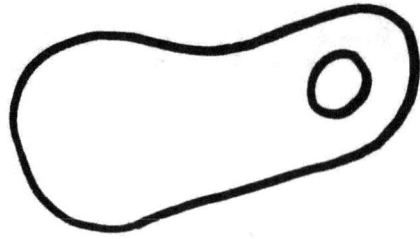

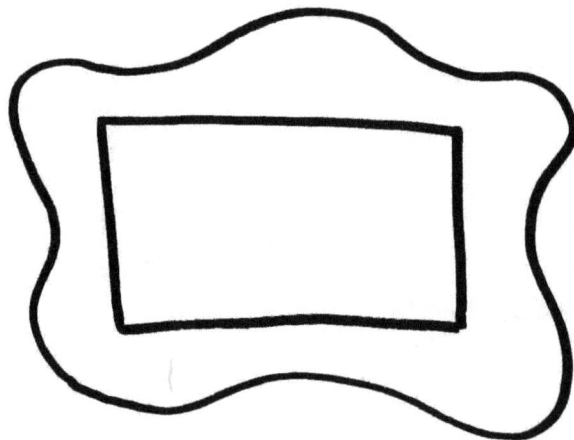

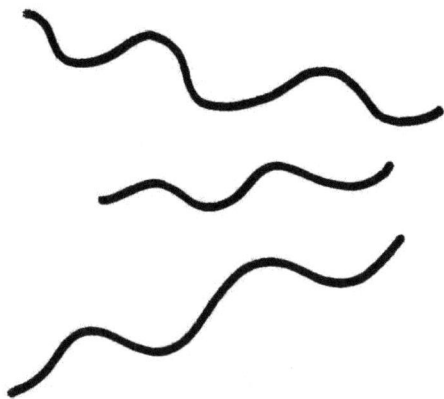

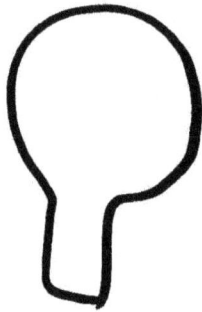

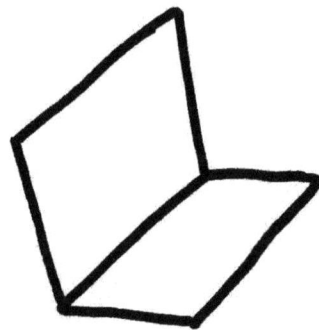

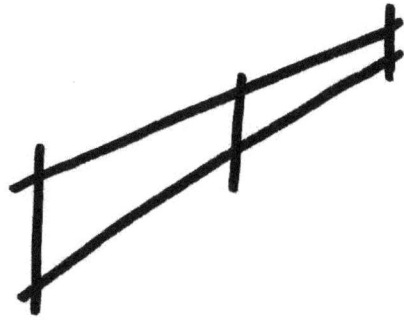

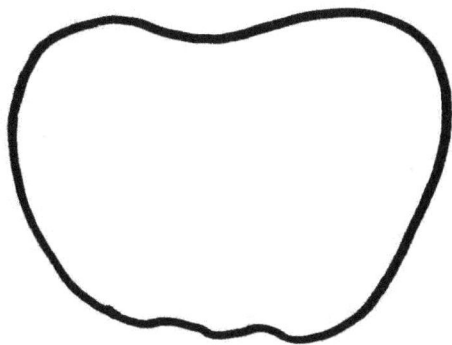

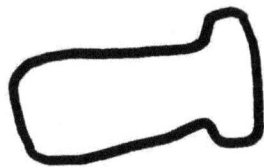

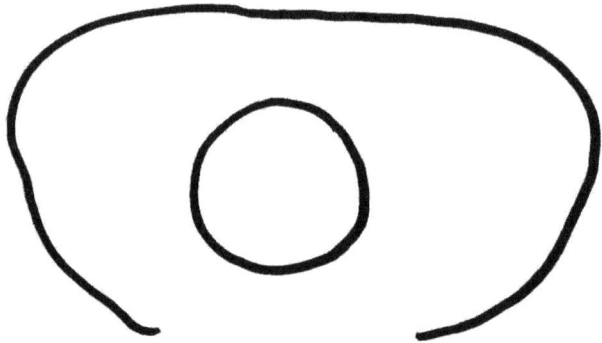

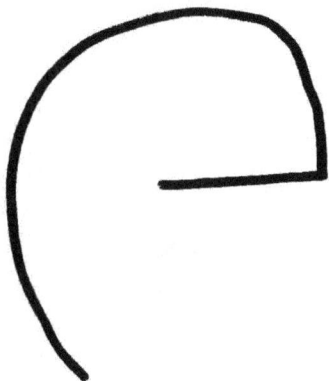

+

---

o

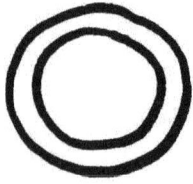

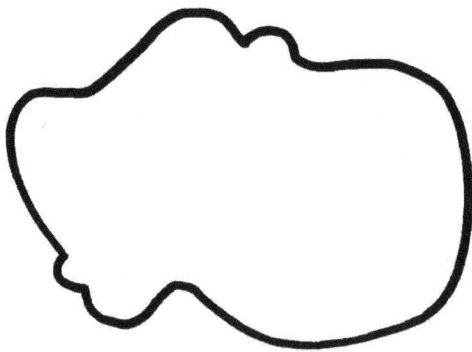

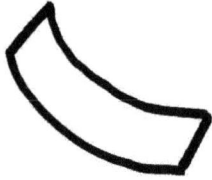

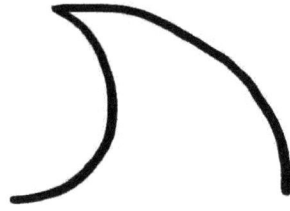

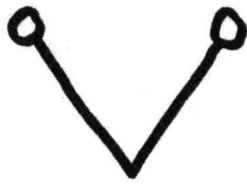

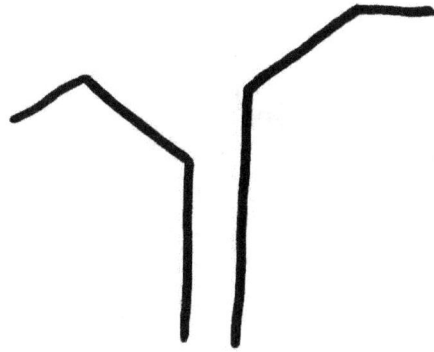

www.ingramcontent.com/pod-product-compliance
Lightning Source LLC
Chambersburg PA
CBHW080935040426
42443CB00015B/3427